NIBBLES

Impressive food to wow your guests

THE AUSTRALIAN
Women's Weekly

contents

Serving finger food to guests instead of a sit-down meal is a great way to entertain, especially if there are a lot of people to feed. The key is to keep the food coming throughout the evening, so be organised, know what can be prepared ahead of time and how many guests to cater for.

Editorial & Food Director

Pamela Clark

Australian cup and spoon measurements are metric. A conversion chart appears on page 77.

light bites

Your guests will feel right at home if you start the party with a choice of delightful appetisers. Keep the buzz going with a celebratory sparkling cocktail.

Tip Serve with Greek-style yoghurt mixed with a pinch of cayenne pepper, if you like.

cauliflower, dill and cumin fritters

- 1 cup (150g) self-raising flour
- ¼ cup (35g) chickpea (besan) flour
- ½ teaspoon cayenne pepper
- 2 tablespoons ground cumin
- 2 teaspoons salt
- ½ cup coarsely chopped fresh dill
- 1 egg, beaten lightly
- 1⅓ cups (330ml) chilled water
- 700g (1½ pounds) cauliflower
- vegetable oil, for deep-frying

1 Combine flours, spices, salt and dill in a medium bowl. Make a well in the centre; add egg and enough of the water to make a smooth batter. Cover, stand 10 minutes.
2 Meanwhile, trim cauliflower into large florets; cut florets into 1cm (½-inch) thick slices.
3 Fill a large saucepan or deep fryer one-third full with oil; heat to 180°C/350°F (or until a cube of bread turns golden in 10 seconds). Dip cauliflower in batter, shaking off excess. Deep fry, in batches, turning halfway through cooking, for 2 minutes or until golden. Remove fritters with a slotted spoon; drain on paper towel.

do-ahead Florets can be cut 3 hours ahead.

makes 40
prep + cook time 30 minutes
nutritional count per fritter
2g total fat (0.3g saturated fat);
162kJ (38 cal); 3.7g carbohydrate;
1.9g protein; 0.6g fibre

roast pumpkin and fetta bruschetta

- 1 long french bread stick (300g)
- cooking-oil spray
- 1.5kg (3-pound) butternut pumpkin
- 1 teaspoon dried chilli flakes
- 1½ teaspoons cumin seeds
- 2 tablespoons extra virgin olive oil
- ½ cup (50g) walnuts, roasted, chopped coarsely
- 180g (5½ ounces) persian fetta, crumbled
- 1 tablespoon fresh thyme leaves

1 Preheat oven to 180°C/350°F. Line two oven trays with baking paper.
2 Trim rounded ends from bread. Cut bread into 30 x 1.5cm (¾-inch) thick slices; spray both sides with cooking oil. Place bread on oven trays. Bake 8 minutes or until browned lightly. Cool on trays.
3 Meanwhile, cut pumpkin lengthways into four slices about 3cm (1¼-inch) thick. Cut each piece into 5mm (¼-inch) thick slices.

4 Place pumpkin, spices and oil in a large bowl; toss well to combine. Arrange slices on two baking paper-lined oven trays. Roast 25 minutes or until just tender.
5 Top bread with 3-4 pumpkin slices; sprinkle over walnuts, fetta and thyme. Drizzle with extra oil, if you like.

do-ahead Bread can be toasted 2 hours ahead; store in an airtight container. Pumpkin can be cooked 1 hour ahead.

makes 30
prep + cook time 50 minutes
nutritional count per piece 4.2g total fat (1.2g saturated fat); 363kJ (86 cal); 8.9g carbohydrate; 2.7g protein; 1.5g fibre

chicken skewers with green olives

- **4 large chicken thigh fillets (800g)**
- **3 cloves garlic, crushed**
- **2 tablespoons finely chopped fresh oregano**
- **2 teaspoons finely grated lemon rind**
- **2 tablespoons strained lemon juice**
- **2 tablespoons olive oil**
- **lemon wedges, to serve**

green olive dressing
- **½ cup (60g) pitted green olives**
- **2 tablespoons fresh oregano leaves**
- **⅓ cup (80ml) olive oil**

1 Cut each thigh fillet into 6 long strips; combine with garlic, oregano, rind, juice and oil in a medium bowl. Cover with plastic wrap, refrigerate 2 hours.

2 Make green olive dressing.

3 Thread one strip of chicken onto each skewer. Cook chicken, in batches, on a heated, oiled grill plate (or grill or barbecue) for 2 minutes each side or until cooked through.

4 Serve chicken skewers with dressing and lemon wedges.

green olive dressing Coarsely chop 4 olives; reserve. Blend or process remaining ingredients until almost smooth. Transfer into a serving bowl; top with chopped olives.

> **tip** An aromatic herb, oregano is a member of the mint family. It has a woody stalk and clumps of tiny, dark-green leaves, with a pungent, peppery flavour.

makes 24
prep + cook time
30 minutes (+ refrigeration)
nutritional count per skewer 9g total fat
(1.9g saturated fat); 487kJ
(116 cal); 5.2g carbohydrate;
3.7g protein; 0.1g fibre

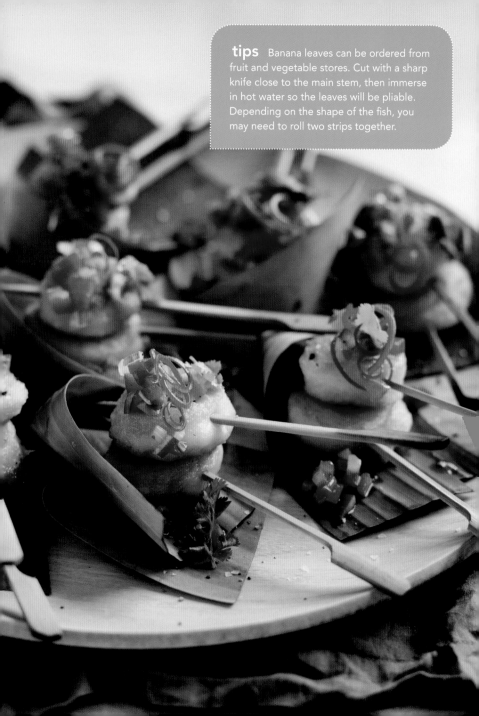

tips Banana leaves can be ordered from fruit and vegetable stores. Cut with a sharp knife close to the main stem, then immerse in hot water so the leaves will be pliable. Depending on the shape of the fish, you may need to roll two strips together.

fish scrolls
with capsicum salsa

You need 30 small (15cm/6-inch) bamboo skewers, and a large banana leaf (see tips).

- **1kg (2-pound) piece firm white fish fillet, skin and bones removed**
- **¼ cup (60ml) red wine vinegar**
- **⅓ cup (80ml) olive oil**
- **½ small red capsicum (bell pepper) (75g), chopped finely**
- **½ small green capsicum (bell pepper) (75g), chopped finely**
- **½ small red onion (50g), chopped finely**
- **1 small tomato (90g), seeded, chopped finely**
- **1 fresh long red chilli, seeded, sliced thinly**
- **fresh coriander leaves (cilantro), to serve**

1 Cut fish into 30 x 12cm (4¾-inch) strips, 1cm (½-inch) thick. Roll each strip into a scroll, secure with a skewer; season.

2 Combine vinegar and oil in a small saucepan; stir over low heat for 3 minutes or until warm, do not boil. Combine capsicum, onion and tomato in a small bowl; pour over warmed vinegar mixture, season to taste.

3 Meanwhile, heat an oiled large frying pan over medium-high heat; pan-fry fish, in batches, for 1½ minutes each side or until just cooked through.

4 Cut banana leaves into large rectangles; serve fish on banana leaves with capsicum salsa. Sprinkle over chilli and coriander.

makes 30
prep + cook time 40 minutes
nutritional count per scroll 3.9g total fat (0.7g saturated fat); 268kJ (64 cal); 0.2g carbohydrate; 6.8g protein; 0.1g fibre

dukkah-crusted lamb with smoked eggplant dip

- 1 tablespoon olive oil
- 2 tablespoons dukkah
- 600g (1¼ pounds) lamb backstraps

eggplant dip

- 1 large eggplant (500g)
- 1 clove garlic, crushed
- 1 teaspoon sea salt flakes
- 1 teaspoon ground cumin
- 1 tablespoon finely chopped fresh flat-leaf parsley
- 2 tablespoons tahini
- ¼ cup (60ml) lemon juice

makes 12
prep + cook time 40 minutes (+ refrigeration & standing)
nutritional count per piece 7.4g total fat (1.6g saturated fat); 517kJ (123 cal); 1.3g carbohydrate; 12.3g protein; 1.4g fibre

1 Combine oil, dukkah and lamb in a medium bowl; cover, refrigerate 2 hours.

2 Meanwhile, make eggplant dip.

3 Stand lamb at room temperature for 15 minutes. Heat an oiled grill plate or frying pan over medium heat. Cook lamb for 3 minutes each side (for medium rare) or until cooked as desired. Cover lamb; rest for 5 minutes before slicing thinly, season.

4 Top 1 tablespoon of dip with 3 slices of lamb. Drizzle with olive oil and serve with fresh flat-leaf parsley sprigs, if you like.

eggplant dip Prick eggplant all over with a fork. Cook over medium heat on an oiled grill plate (or grill or barbecue) for 25 minutes, turning frequently, or until tender. When cool enough to handle, peel eggplant. Squeeze eggplant flesh to remove any excess juice. Blend or process eggplant with remaining ingredients until smooth. Season to taste.

do-ahead Eggplant dip can be made a day ahead; store, covered, in the fridge. Lamb can be marinated a day ahead; store, covered, in the fridge.

Tip Dukkah is a packaged spice and nut blend; it is available from spice shops, major supermarkets and delis.

Sparkling

champagne sidecar

Place 20ml brandy, 20ml cointreau, 20ml lemon juice and 15ml sugar syrup (see tip) in a chilled 230ml champagne flute glass; stir gently. Top with 150ml chilled dry white sparkling wine. Garnish with strawberry slices.

tip To make sugar syrup, stir 1 cup caster (superfine) sugar with 1 cup of water in a small saucepan over low heat, until sugar dissolves; bring to the boil. Reduce heat; simmer, uncovered, 5 minutes. Cool. Refrigerate in an airtight container for up to 1 month.

lychee and raspberry fizz

Place one sugar cube in each hole of two 12-hole ice-cube trays; stain each cube with two drops of Angostura bitters. Strain 560g (1 pound) canned lychees in syrup over a bowl, reserve syrup; quarter lychees. Divide lychees and 125g (4 ounces) raspberries into ice-cube trays. Combine reserved lychee syrup and 1 cup of chilled water; pour into trays; freeze for 4 hours. Unmould ice cubes into a chilled bowl. To serve, place two ice cubes into each cocktail glass, top with 1 teaspoon brandy; pour in chilled prosecco. Serve immediately.

serves 1
prep time 5 minutes

serves 12
prep time 15 minutes (+ freezing)

bellini

Place 45ml peach nectar, 15ml peach schnapps and 5ml lime juice in a chilled 230ml champagne flute glass; stir gently. Top with 150ml chilled dry white sparkling wine. Garnish with a peach wedge.

scroppino with strawberry purée

Blend or process 375g (12 ounces) chopped strawberries and ¼ cup elderflower cordial until smooth. Transfer to a jug; refrigerate until needed. To make the scroppino, blend ⅓ cup chilled vodka, 750ml chilled prosecco and 3 litres (12 cups) lemon sorbet in two batches until combined. Pour 1 tablespoon strawberry purée into the base of each chilled glass, top with scroppino. Serve immediately.

serves 1
prep time 5 minutes

serves 12
prep time 15 minutes (+ refrigeration)

makes 30
prep + cook time
45 minutes (+ standing)
nutritional count per prawn
0.9g total fat (0.1g saturated fat);
188kJ (45 cal); 6.2g carbohydrate;
3.1g protein; 0.1g fibre

salt and pepper prawns with sweet chilli syrup

- 30 uncooked medium prawns (shrimp) (800g)
- ¾ cup (55g) japanese breadcrumbs (panko)
- 1 teaspoon cracked black peppercorns
- 1½ teaspoons piri piri seasoning
- 2 teaspoons sea salt flakes
- 1 egg white, beaten lightly
- vegetable oil, for deep-frying
- 1 fresh long red chilli, sliced thinly
- 2 tablespoons fresh coriander leaves (cilantro)

sweet chilli syrup

- ½ cup (110g) white (granulated) sugar
- ½ cup (125ml) water
- ¼ cup (80g) sweet chilli sauce
- 4 kaffir lime leaves, torn
- 5g (¼ ounce) piece fresh ginger, sliced thinly
- 2 fresh coriander (cilantro) roots and stems, washed, sliced thinly

1 Make sweet chilli syrup.
2 Shell and devein prawns leaving tails intact.
3 Combine crumbs, pepper, seasoning and salt in a small bowl. Holding prawns by the tail, dip into egg white, then coat in crumb mixture.
4 Fill a large saucepan or deep fryer one-third full with oil; heat to 180°C/350°F (or until a cube of bread turns golden in 10 seconds). Deep fry prawns, in batches, for 1 minute or until cooked through and crisp. Remove with a slotted spoon; drain on paper towel.
5 Sprinkle prawns with chilli and coriander leaves; serve with sweet chilli syrup for dipping.

sweet chilli syrup
Combine ingredients in a small saucepan; stir over medium heat until sugar dissolves. Bring to the boil; reduce heat, simmer, uncovered, about 5 minutes or until sauce thickens slightly. Remove from heat; stand 15 minutes, then discard lime leaves.

do-ahead Syrup can be made up to 2 days ahead; store, covered, in the fridge. Prawns can be crumbed 3 hours ahead; store, covered, in the fridge.

Tip The trick to tidy-looking sandwiches is to cut them using a fast sawing action, without applying pressure.

chicken and almond sandwiches

- 2½ cups (400g) finely chopped, boneless, skinless cooked chicken
- ½ cup (120g) sour cream
- ½ cup (150g) whole-egg mayonnaise
- 2 stalks celery (300g), trimmed, chopped finely
- ½ cup (40g) flaked almonds, toasted
- 50g (1½ ounces) baby rocket leaves (arugula), chopped coarsely
- 18 large slices wholegrain bread (810g)

1 Combine chicken, sour cream, mayonnaise, celery, nuts and rocket in a large bowl. Season to taste.

2 Sandwich chicken mixture equally between bread slices.

3 Using a sharp serrated knife (or electric knife), trim crusts; cut sandwiches into quarters.

do-ahead Chicken filling can be made, without the nuts, 3 hours ahead; store, covered, in the fridge. Bring filling to room temperature then add the nuts just before assembling sandwiches to retain their crunch.

makes 36
prep time 25 minutes
nutritional count per sandwich 6.1g total fat (1.4g saturated fat); 409kJ (98 cal); 5.2g carbohydrate; 5g protein; 0.9g fibre

haloumi and avocado bruschetta

- 400g (12½-ounce) loaf afghan bread
- cooking-oil spray
- 500g (1 pound) haloumi cheese
- 3 medium avocados (750g), chopped coarsely
- 1 medium red onion (170g), chopped finely
- 2 medium tomatoes (300g), chopped finely
- 1 tablespoon olive oil
- 2 tablespoons lemon juice
- 40g (1½ ounces) baby rocket leaves (arugula)

makes 24
prep + cook time 30 minutes
nutritional count per piece 11g total fat (4.3g saturated fat); 720kJ (172 cal) 10.2g carbohydrate 7.3g protein; 0.9g fibre

1 Preheat oven to 180°C/350°F. Line two oven trays with baking paper.
2 Trim rounded edges from bread to form a 16cm x 48cm (6½-inch x 19¼-inch) rectangle. Level top of bread; discard trimmings. Cut bread into 24 rectangles 4cm x 8cm long (1½-inch x 3¼-inch); spray both sides with cooking oil.
3 Place bread, cut-side up, on oven trays; bake 6 minutes or until browned lightly.
4 Cut haloumi into 24 thin slices; lay between 2 sheets of paper towel for 5 minutes.

5 Meanwhile, combine avocado, onion, tomato, oil and juice in a medium bowl. Season to taste.
6 Pan-fry haloumi, in batches, in an oiled large frying pan, for 1 minute each side or until browned.
7 Top bread with one slice of haloumi, some avocado mixture and a few rocket leaves to serve.

do-ahead Toast bread 2 hours ahead; store in an airtight container. Combine avocado mixture 1 hour ahead; store, covered, in the fridge. Haloumi is best cooked just before serving.

tomato, fetta and pancetta frittata

- 6 slices (100g) pancetta, chopped coarsely
- 100g (3 ounces) fetta cheese, crumbled
- ¼ cup (20g) finely grated parmesan
- ⅓ cup coarsely chopped fresh basil leaves
- 6 eggs
- ⅔ cup (160ml) cream
- 9 mini roma tomatoes (150g), halved lengthways

1 Preheat oven to 180°C/350°F. Oil a six-hole (¾-cup/180ml) texas muffin pan; line bases with baking paper.
2 Layer pancetta, cheeses and basil in pan holes. Whisk eggs and cream in a medium bowl; pour into pan holes. Top each frittata with three tomato halves.
3 Bake about 25 minutes. Stand in pan 5 minutes before turning out. Sprinkle over extra fresh small basil leaves to serve, if you like.

makes 6
prep + cooking time 35 minutes
nutritional count per frittata 24.1g total fat (13.3g saturated fat); 1170kJ (280 cal); 1.6g carbohydrate; 14.9g protein; 0.4g fibre

tips You could substitute vodka for gin or omit the alcohol completely. Micro herbs are small punnets of various baby herbs or cress; alternatively, use the smallest torn leaves from a regular bunch of herbs.

gravlax

Start this recipe the day before.

- ½ cup (150g) rock salt
- ½ cup (110g) white (granulated) sugar
- ⅔ cup coarsely chopped fresh dill
- 2 teaspoons finely grated lime rind
- 2 teaspoons white peppercorns, crushed
- 1 tablespoon juniper berries, crushed
- ⅓ cup (80ml) gin
- 750g (1½-pound) centre-cut piece salmon fillet, skin-on, bones removed
- 2 tablespoons lime juice
- 2 tablespoons olive oil

herb salad
- 2 punnets micro herbs, trimmed
- ¼ cup fresh dill sprigs

1 Combine salt, sugar, dill, rind, pepper, berries and gin in a medium bowl. Spread half the gin mixture over the base of a shallow 20cm x 28cm (8-inch x 11¼-inch) ceramic or glass dish. Place salmon, skin-side down, over mixture. Top with remaining gin mixture.
2 Cover with plastic wrap. Place another dish on top, weigh down with cans of food. Refrigerate 24-36 hours, turning salmon every 12 hours.
3 Remove salmon from dish; scraping away any loose mixture, discard gin mixture. Pat salmon dry with paper towel.

4 Holding a knife at a 45 degree angle, slice salmon across the grain as thinly as possible using long strokes. Arrange slices on a large platter.
5 Just before serving, make herb salad.
6 Drizzle salmon with juice and oil; top with herb salad. Serve with crème fraîche and toasted french bread stick, pumpernickel bread or crackers, if you like.
herb salad Combine herbs in a small bowl.

serves 12
prep time 30 minutes (+ refrigeration)
nutritional count per serving 10.9g total fat (2.5g saturated fat) 744kJ (177 cal); 1.4g carbohydrate; 17.8g protein; 0g fibre

tuna tartare

- cooking-oil spray
- 36 square wonton wrappers
- 600g (1¼ pounds) sashimi-grade tuna, chopped finely
- 2 teaspoons finely grated lemon rind
- 2 tablespoons finely chopped cornichons
- 2 tablespoons finely chopped fresh flat-leaf parsley
- 2 tablespoons finely chopped fresh chives
- 2 tablespoons olive oil
- 3 shallots (75g), chopped finely
- 4 drained anchovy fillets, chopped finely
- ¼ cup (50g) rinsed, drained baby capers
- 2 tablespoons strained lemon juice
- ¼ cup trimmed fresh micro cress or finely chopped fresh parsley leaves or chives, extra, to serve
- finely grated lemon rind, extra, to serve

1 Preheat oven to 180°C/350°F. Spray three 12-hole (1-tablespoon/20ml) mini muffin pans with cooking oil. Press one wrapper into each pan hole; spray with cooking oil. Bake 7 minutes or until browned lightly and crisp. Cool on a wire rack.

2 Meanwhile, combine tuna, rind, cornichons, herbs, oil, shallots, anchovy and capers in a medium bowl. Season to taste.

3 Just before serving, stir juice into tuna mixture. Spoon mixture into wonton cups; top with cress and extra lemon rind, to serve.

do-ahead Wonton cups can be prepared a day ahead and stored in an airtight container.

makes 36
prep + cook time
30 minutes (+ cooling)
nutritional count per piece 1.4g total fat (0.2g saturated fat); 215kJ (51 cal); 4.3g carbohydrate; 23.8g protein; 0.1g fibre

tips If you only have one pan, just cook the wonton cases in batches. You could also serve the tuna tartare in a bowl with a pile of home-cooked prawn crackers for guests to assemble themselves.

hearty

As the party progresses, move onto more substantial fare. Provide the familiar favourites but also try your hand at quesadillas and quail eggs.

eggplant and prosciutto pizza

- 2 cloves garlic, crushed
- 1 tablespoon olive oil
- 2 x 20cm x 30cm (8-inch x 12-inch) rectangular pizza bases (440g)
- 350g (11 ounces) drained char-grilled eggplant
- 200g (6½ ounces) bocconcini cheese, torn
- 250g (8 ounces) cherry tomatoes
- 100g (3 ounces) thinly sliced prosciutto, chopped coarsely
- 40g (1½ ounces) baby rocket leaves (arugula)
- 2 teaspoons olive oil, extra
- 1 teaspoon balsamic vinegar

1 Preheat oven to 240°C/475°F. Oil two oven trays; place in heated oven.

2 Combine garlic and oil in a small bowl. Place pizza bases on trays; brush with oil mixture. Top with eggplant, cheese and tomatoes; season.

3 Bake pizzas for 15 minutes or until bases are browned and crisp. Serve topped with prosciutto and rocket. Drizzle with combined extra oil and vinegar.

serves 4
prep + cook time 30 minutes
nutritional count per serving 22.2g total fat (7.3g saturated fat); 2830kJ (677 cal); 84.9g carbohydrate; 28.8g protein; 10.5g fibre

makes 24
prep + cook time 50 minutes
nutritional count per pie
12.1g total fat (5.4g saturated fat);
842kJ (201 cal); 15.5g carbohydrate;
7.4g protein; 0.6g fibre

beef and onion party pies

- 1 tablespoon vegetable oil
- 1 medium brown onion (150g), chopped finely
- 450g (14½ ounces) minced (ground) beef
- 2 tablespoons tomato paste
- 2 tablespoons worcestershire sauce
- 2 tablespoons powdered gravy mix
- ¾ cup (180ml) water
- 3 sheets ready-rolled shortcrust pastry
- 1 egg, beaten lightly
- 2 sheets ready-rolled puff pastry
- 1 tablespoon sesame seeds

1 Heat oil in a large frying pan over medium-high heat; cook onion, stirring, for 4 minutes or until onion softens. Add beef; cook, stirring, until beef changes colour. Add paste, sauce, and blended gravy powder and the water; bring to the boil, stirring. Reduce heat; simmer, uncovered, for 10 minutes or until thickened slightly; cool.

2 Preheat oven to 200°C/400°F. Oil two 12-hole (2-tablespoons/40ml) deep flat-based patty pans.

3 Cut 24 x 7cm (2¾-inch) rounds from shortcrust pastry; press into pan holes. Divide beef mixture among pastry cases. Brush edges with a little of the egg.

4 Cut 24 x 6cm (2½-inch) rounds from puff pastry; top pies with puff pastry lids. Press edges firmly to seal; brush lids with remaining egg. Sprinkle with sesame seeds, cut a small slit in the lid of each pie.

5 Bake for 20 minutes or until browned lightly. Stand pies in pan 5 minutes before serving.

chicken, jalapeño and cheese quesadillas

- 2 cups (320g) shredded, skinless barbecue chicken
- 1 cup (120g) finely grated cheddar
- 1 cup (100g) finely grated mozzarella
- ¼ cup (50g) drained, finely chopped pickled jalapeño chillies
- ½ medium red onion (85g), sliced thinly
- 16 x 15cm (6-inch) mini corn or flour tortillas
- ¼ cup (60ml) olive oil
- ¾ cup (90g) finely grated cheddar, extra
- 2 medium avocados (500g), chopped coarsely
- 2 tablespoons lime juice
- ⅓ cup loosely packed fresh coriander leaves (cilantro)

1 Preheat oven to 180°C/350°F. Line a large oven tray with baking paper.

2 Combine chicken, cheeses, chilli and onion in a large bowl; season to taste. Fold tortilla into quarters. Holding folded tortilla like a cone; divide filling among tortillas. Place a toothpick into the base of each tortilla to hold it closed, if necessary; place on oven tray.

3 Brush quesadillas with oil; sprinkle over extra cheese. Bake 12 minutes or until golden and heated through.

4 Meanwhile, combine avocado and juice in a bowl; season to taste. Sprinkle with coriander.

5 Serve quesadillas on a platter, each topped with a tablespoon of the avocado mixture.

makes 16
prep + cook time 30 minutes
nutritional count per piece 17.2g total fat (6.9g saturated fat); 1098kJ (262 cal); 14.1g carbohydrate; 12.3g protein; 0.8g fibre

tips Serve with Greek-style yoghurt, tomato chutney or tomato sauce flavoured with a little pomegranate molasses and a pinch of ground allspice. Middle-Eastern spice blend is available from supermarkets. Substitute with 1 tablespoon each ground cumin and coriander mixed with ½ teaspoon each ground turmeric and cardamom.

middle-eastern sausage rolls

- **4 shallots (100g), chopped finely**
- **3 cloves garlic, crushed**
- **1kg (2 pounds) minced (ground) lamb**
- **2 tablespoons tomato paste**
- **½ cup (50g) packaged breadcrumbs**
- **½ cup (70g) pistachios, chopped coarsely**
- **¼ cup finely chopped fresh coriander (cilantro)**
- **¼ cup (32g) middle-eastern spice blend**
- **3 teaspoons fennel seeds**
- **3 eggs**
- **4 sheets puff pastry**
- **sea salt flakes, for sprinkling**

makes 32
prep + cook time
45 minutes (+ refrigeration)
nutritional count per roll
11.7g total fat
(5.2g saturated fat);
799kJ (190 cal);
11.4g carbohydrate;
9.6g protein; 0.7g fibre

1 Place shallot, garlic, lamb, paste, breadcrumbs, pistachios, coriander, spice blend, 1 teaspoon of the fennel seeds and 2 eggs in a large bowl, season; mix well to combine. Cover; refrigerate for 3 hours to allow flavours to develop.
2 Preheat oven to 200°C/400°F. Line oven trays with baking paper.
3 Beat remaining egg lightly. Cut pastry in half; fill a large piping bag with lamb mixture, pipe lamb mixture down one long edge of the pastry. Brush the opposite long edge with beaten egg; roll tightly to enclose. Repeat with remaining pastry, lamb mixture and egg.

4 Score pastry at ½cm (⅛-inch) intervals. Brush rolls with beaten egg; cut each roll into four pieces, sprinkle with salt and remaining fennel seeds.
5 Place rolls, seam-side down, on oven trays; bake for 25 minutes or until golden and cooked through. Serve immediately.

do-ahead Sausage rolls can be made and frozen in advance. Allow about an extra 5 minutes when baking from frozen.

quail eggs with spiced salt

- 1½ teaspoons celery seeds
- 1 teaspoon cumin seeds
- 1 teaspoon fennel seeds
- ½ teaspoon sumac
- 3 teaspoons brown sugar
- 1 teaspoon sea salt flakes
- 24 quail eggs

1 Place celery, cumin and fennel seeds in a saucepan over medium heat. Cook, stirring frequently, 2 minutes or until fragrant. Using a mortar and pestle, grind seed mixture to a powder. Cool completely; stir in sumac, sugar and salt.

2 Place eggs in a medium saucepan of boiling water; cook 2½ minutes for soft-boiled eggs or 3 minutes for hard-boiled. Drain; refresh in iced water. For easier peeling, peel eggs while still slightly warm.

3 Scatter salt mixture evenly over a tray, roll quail eggs in salt.

4 Sprinkle trimmed baby lamb's lettuce over the eggs to serve, if you like.

tip Quail eggs are available from selected butchers and delicatessens. Alternatively, place an order with your local butcher a few days in advance.

makes 24
prep + cook time 15 minutes
nutritional count per egg
1.1g total fat (0g saturated fat);
72kJ (17 cal); 0.6g carbohydrate;
1.1g protein; 1g fibre

makes 20
prep + cook time
25 minutes (+ refrigeration)
nutritional count per cutlet
17g total fat (4.3g saturated fat);
747kJ (179 cal); 1g carbohydrate;
5.5g protein; 0.7g fibre

Tips If you are pressed for time, process all the chimichurri ingredients in a food processor until coarsely chopped. You can substitute chicken wings or drumsticks for the lamb cutlets, if you prefer.

chimichurri lamb cutlets

- 4 fresh long red chillies, seeded, chopped finely
- 3 cloves garlic, crushed
- 2 tablespoons red wine vinegar
- 2 teaspoons each dried oregano, ground cumin and sweet paprika
- 1 large tomato (220g), chopped finely
- 1 large red onion (200g), chopped finely
- ½ cup firmly packed fresh flat-leaf parsley leaves, shredded finely
- 1 cup (250ml) extra virgin olive oil
- 20 frenched lamb cutlets (1kg)

1 To make chimichurri, place all ingredients except lamb in a large bowl, season; stir to combine.

2 Transfer half the chimichurri to a large bowl with lamb; toss to coat. Cover; refrigerate 3 hours or overnight. Cover remaining chimichurri; refrigerate until required.

3 Preheat a grill pan (or barbecue) over high heat. Cook lamb, turning occasionally, for 4 minutes (for medium) or until cooked to your liking. Cover lamb; rest for 5 minutes.

4 Place lamb cutlets on a large platter; serve with reserved chimichurri. Sprinkle over extra fresh parsley sprigs to serve, if you like.

Mocktails

moroccan mint tea

Combine 1 litre hot water, 3 black tea bags
and 1 cup loosely packed fresh mint leaves
in a medium jug; stand 10 minutes. Discard
tea bags, cover; refrigerate until cool. Strain
tea mixture into a medium jug; discard
leaves. Stir in 2 tablespoons caster sugar,
½ cup fresh mint leaves and 1 cup ice cubes.

lemon grass and lime spritzer

Place ⅓ cup grated palm sugar and ½ cup
water in a small saucepan; stir, over low heat,
until sugar dissolves. Remove from heat; stir
in 2 tablespoons coarsely chopped fresh
lemon grass. Cover; refrigerate until chilled.
Combine strained sugar mixture with ½ cup
lime juice, 750ml chilled sparkling mineral
water and 1 cup ice cubes in a large jug.

makes 1 litre (4 cups)
prep time 10 minutes (+ refrigeration)

makes 1 litre (4 cups)
prep + cook time 15 minutes (+ refrigeration)

virgin sea breeze

Place 2 cups chilled cranberry juice,
2 cups chilled ruby red grapefruit juice
and 2 tablespoons lime juice in a large
jug; stir to combine.

watermelon refresher

Blend or process 900g (1¾ pounds)
coarsely chopped seedless watermelon,
½ cup chilled orange juice and 2 tablespoons
lime juice until smooth. Garnish with lime
slices, if you like.

tip You will need a 1.5kg piece
of watermelon for this recipe.

makes 1 litre (4 cups)
prep time 5 minutes

makes 1 litre (4 cups)
prep time 10 minutes

Tip To serve, sprinkle with lemon salt: combine ½ cup sea salt flakes, the thinly sliced rind of 2 lemons and 2 tablespoons finely chopped fresh lemon thyme.

fried buttermilk and mustard chicken wings

- 1 cup (300g) rock salt
- 1 cup (220g) firmly packed brown sugar
- 2 tablespoons finely grated lemon rind
- 2 tablespoons finely chopped fresh lemon thyme
- 1 clove garlic, crushed
- 1.5kg (3 pounds) chicken wing nibbles
- ¾ cup (105g) plain (all-purpose) flour, plus extra, to dust
- 600ml buttermilk
- 2 tablespoons hot english mustard
- 1 egg, beaten lightly
- vegetable oil, for deep-frying

1 Place salt, sugar, rind, thyme and garlic in a large bowl; mix to combine. Add chicken, toss well to coat; cover, refrigerate 1 hour.

2 Wash salt mixture from chicken under cold water; pat chicken dry with paper towel.

3 Place flour in a large bowl; gradually whisk in combined buttermilk, mustard and egg. Season.

4 Fill a large saucepan or deep fryer one-third full with oil; heat to 180°C/350°F (or until a cube of bread turns golden in 10 seconds).

5 Dust chicken in extra flour. Dip chicken into batter; shaking off excess. Deep fry, in batches, turning halfway through cooking, for 6 minutes or until golden and cooked through. Remove chicken with a slotted spoon; drain on paper towel.

serves 12
prep + cook time
40 minutes
(+ refrigeration)
nutritional count per serving 15.6g total fat (3.7g saturated fat); 1055kJ (252 cal); 12.1g carbohydrate; 16g protein; 0.2g fibre

polenta, blue cheese and fig tarts

- 2 cups (500ml) milk
- ½ cup (80g) instant polenta
- ½ cup (40g) finely grated parmesan
- 2 tablespoons finely chopped fresh chives
- 24 x 6cm (2½-inch) small tart shells (220g)
- 12 small fresh figs (600g), halved lengthways
- 150g (5 ounces) blue cheese, crumbled
- ½ cup loosely packed fresh chervil sprigs
- ¼ cup (60ml) balsamic glaze

makes 24
prep + cook time 20 minutes
nutritional count per tart 5.6g total fat (3.3g saturated fat); 486kJ (116 cal); 11.7g carbohydrate; 3.9g protein; 0.8g fibre

1 To make polenta, place milk in a small, heavy-based saucepan over medium heat; bring to a simmer. Whisking continuously, gradually add polenta in a thin stream; whisk for 5 minutes or until cooked and thickened. Remove from heat; stir in parmesan and chives. Season to taste.

2 Place 1 tablespoon of polenta into each tart shell. (If the polenta has thickened too much on standing, thin it by gradually whisking in a little extra milk.) Top with fig halves; sprinkle over blue cheese.

3 Place tarts on a large platter; top with chervil, drizzle with balsamic glaze.

tip Blue cheese refers to cheeses made from cow's milk, sheep's milk, or goat's milk that have had various specially cultivated bacteria added.

smoked ocean trout and pickled fennel buns

- 20 medium bread rolls (1kg), halved
- 1 cup (240g) spreadable cream cheese
- 480g (15½ ounces) hot-smoked ocean trout, flaked
- 2 baby cos lettuce (360g), leaves separated
- 4 small red radishes (140g), sliced thinly
- 1 small red onion (100g), sliced thinly into rings

pickled fennel

- ⅓ cup (80ml) strained lemon juice
- 2 tablespoons caster (superfine) sugar
- 2 tablespoons finely chopped fresh dill
- 1 tablespoon mustard seeds, toasted
- 1 tablespoon white wine vinegar
- 2 teaspoons sea salt flakes
- 4 baby fennel bulbs (520g), trimmed, sliced thinly
- ¼ cup (60ml) extra virgin olive oil

1 Make pickled fennel.
2 Spread bread roll bases with cream cheese; layer with trout, lettuce, pickled fennel, radish and onion. Top with bread roll lids.
3 Serve buns immediately on a large platter.

pickled fennel Whisk juice, sugar, dill, seeds, vinegar and salt until sugar dissolves. Add fennel, season to taste; toss to combine. Cover; refrigerate 30 minutes to allow flavours to develop. Drain and discard pickling liquid, then toss pickled fennel with oil.

tips Use a mandoline or V-slicer, available from kitchenware and department stores, to slice the fennel and radishes. Substitute salmon fillets for the ocean trout, if you prefer. For decoration and ease of handling either tie the rolls with kitchen string or secure them with toothpicks.

makes 20
prep time 20 minutes
(+ refrigeration)
nutritional count per
bun 10g total fat
(3.6g saturated fat); 1080kJ
(258 cal); 3.6g carbohydrate;
14.9g protein; 0.8g fibre

makes 30
prep + cook time
35 minutes (+ refrigeration)
nutritional count per prawn
1.8g total fat (0.3g saturated fat);
397kJ (95 cal); 14.2g carbohydrate;
5.7g protein; 0.1g fibre

Tip Tempura batter mix is available in the spice and sauce aisle at larger supermarkets.

tempura prawns with lime and chilli sauce

- 1 cup (220g) caster (superfine) sugar
- ¼ cup (60ml) chinese cooking wine
- 1 lebanese cucumber (130g), seeded, chopped finely
- 2 fresh long red chillies, seeded, sliced thinly
- 2 tablespoons rice wine vinegar
- 1 tablespoon sesame oil
- 2 tablespoons lime juice
- 1 teaspoon finely grated lime rind
- 250g (8 ounces) tempura batter mix
- 1¾ cups (330ml) chilled sparkling water
- vegetable oil, for deep-frying
- 30 medium green king prawns (1.5kg), shelled and deveined, tails intact

1 Place sugar and wine in a small saucepan over medium heat. Bring to a simmer; cook, stirring, for 5 minutes or until sugar dissolves. Remove from heat; cool slightly. Stir in cucumber and chilli; refrigerate until cooled completely. Stir in vinegar, oil, juice and rind.

2 Meanwhile, place tempura mix in a large bowl, season; gradually whisk in sparkling water.

3 Fill a large saucepan or deep fryer one-third full with oil; heat to 180°C/350°F (or until a cube of bread turns golden in 10 seconds). Dip prawns into batter, shaking off excess. Deep fry, in batches, turning halfway through cooking, for 5 minutes or until golden. Remove prawns with a slotted spoon; drain on paper towel.

4 Serve prawns with lime and chilli sauce.

Tip *Substitute sliced prosciutto or ham for the pancetta, if you prefer.*

croque monsieur baguette

- 1 french bread stick (500g)
- 80g (1½ ounces) butter, softened
- ½ cup (125g) dijon mustard
- 12 slices pancetta (180g)
- 150g (5 ounces) thinly sliced gruyère cheese
- 12 baby cornichons, drained

makes 12
prep + cook time 15 minutes
nutritional count per baguette 9.1g total fat (4.6g saturated fat); 981kJ (234 cal); 26.7g carbohydrate; 10.4g protein; 1.8g fibre

1 Using a serrated knife, cut the bread crossways into 24 slices.
2 Brush one side of each slice with butter; turn slices buttered-side down. Spread tops of all slices with mustard; top half the slices with pancetta and cheese, sandwich with remaining slices keeping the buttered side on the outside.
3 Preheat a large sandwich press. Toast baguettes for 5 minutes or until golden and cheese is melted.
4 Top each baguette with a cornichon, secure with a toothpick.

do-ahead Baguettes can be made 4 hours ahead: store, covered, in the fridge. Reheat on a baking paper-lined oven tray in a 180°C/350°F oven for 6 minutes or until heated through.

makes 24
prep + cook time
30 minutes (+ refrigeration)
nutritional count per skewer 2.3g total fat
(0.4g saturated fat); 407kJ
(97 cal); 7.1g carbohydrate;
11.5g protein; 0g fibre

chicken yakitori

You need 24 x 15cm (6-inch) bamboo skewers.

- 2 tablespoons jasmine rice
- ⅓ cup (80ml) tamari or soy sauce
- ¼ cup (60ml) sake
- ¼ cup (60ml) mirin
- ½ cup (110g) caster (superfine) sugar
- 2 teaspoons chinese five-spice
- 2 tablespoons finely grated orange rind
- 2 tablespoons grapeseed oil
- 24 chicken tenderloins (1.2kg)
- 2 green onions (scallions), sliced thinly diagonally

1 Heat a medium frying pan over medium heat. Add rice; toast, stirring frequently, for 5 minutes or until fragrant and light golden. Transfer to a mortar and pestle; pound until finely ground.

2 Place tamari, sake, mirin, sugar and spice in a small saucepan over medium heat. Bring to a simmer; cook 2 minutes or until sugar dissolves. Remove from heat, add rind and oil. Transfer to a small bowl; refrigerate marinade until cool.

3 Combine tenderloins with marinade; refrigerate 3 hours or overnight.

4 Preheat a barbecue or grill pan over high heat. Drain chicken tenderloins from marinade; reserve marinade in a small bowl. Thread one tenderloin onto each skewer in an 'S' shape. Cook skewers, brushing with reserved marinade, for 8 minutes, turning frequently, until chicken is charred and cooked through.

5 To serve, place skewers on a platter, sprinkle over toasted rice and green onions.

do-ahead Chicken can be marinated and skewered a day ahead.

little boxes

Seek out beautiful serving options for these undeniably cute portions. Everyone will be talking about the novelty of having their very own party favour.

tip Substitute watercress and tatsoi leaves for baby spinach and mizuna, if preferred.

poached ocean trout salad with japanese dressing

- 1½ cups (375ml) fish stock
- 2 cups (500ml) water
- 4 x 200g (6½ ounces) skinless ocean trout fillets
- 340g (11 ounces) asparagus, trimmed, sliced thickly diagonally
- 160g (5 ounces) green beans, trimmed, cut into 2cm (¾-inch) lengths
- 2 tablespoons sesame seeds
- 1 medium telegraph (hothouse) cucumber (400g), halved, seeded, sliced thinly diagonally
- 500g (1 pound) small red radishes, trimmed, sliced thinly
- 200g (6½ ounces) baby spinach leaves
- 200g (6½ ounces) mizuna leaves

japanese dressing

- 1½ tablespoons finely grated fresh ginger
- ¼ cup (60ml) olive oil
- 2 tablespoons lime juice
- ¼ cup (60ml) mirin
- ¼ cup (60ml) soy sauce
- 1 tablespoon finely grated palm sugar
- 1 small red thai (serrano) chilli, chopped finely

1 Place stock and the water in a medium saucepan; bring to the boil over medium heat. Reduce heat to a simmer, add fish fillets; cook for 8 minutes or until almost cooked through. Using a slotted spoon, transfer fish to a plate; cool 5 minutes.

2 Meanwhile, return poaching liquid to the boil, add asparagus and beans; cook for 30 seconds or until asparagus is just tender. Drain; refresh in iced water, then drain again.

3 Make japanese dressing.

4 Place sesame seeds in a small frying pan over medium heat; stir continuously for 2 minutes or until golden. Remove from heat immediately.

5 Place cucumber and radish in a large bowl; add spinach, mizuna and vegetables. Flake fish, add to salad; drizzle with japanese dressing. Divide salad among 20 x 1-cup boxes or containers. Sprinkle with sesame seeds to serve, if you like.

japanese dressing Combine ingredients in a small screw-top jar; shake well.

do-ahead Recipe can be prepared 8 hours ahead to the end of step 4; store, covered, in the fridge.

serves 20
prep + cook time 35 minutes
nutritional count per serving 7.9g total fat (1.8g saturated fat); 560kJ (134 cal); 3.7g carbohydrate; 10.8g protein; 1.4g fibre

potato and pork sausage salad

- 1 whole bulb garlic
- 2 tablespoons olive oil
- 1kg (2 pounds) mixed baby red and yellow potatoes, unpeeled, sliced thinly
- 2 tablespoons white wine vinegar
- 500g (1 pound) pork and fennel sausages
- 1 cup (300g) whole-egg mayonnaise
- 2 tablespoons lemon juice
- ½ cup (50g) rinsed, drained baby capers
- 100g (3 ounces) cornichons, chopped finely
- 4 shallots (100g), sliced thinly
- 1 cup loosely packed fresh flat-leaf parsley, coarsely chopped
- ⅓ cup coarsely chopped fresh dill

serves 12
prep + cook time 45 minutes
nutritional count per serving 33.4g total fat (8.5g saturated fat); 1707kJ (408 cal); 15.5g carbohydrate; 9.9g protein; 3.7g fibre

1 Preheat oven to 200°C/400°F.

2 Place garlic in a small shallow baking dish; drizzle with half the oil. Roast garlic for 20 minutes.

3 Meanwhile, boil, steam or microwave potato until just tender. Drain, transfer to a large heatproof bowl; sprinkle with vinegar. Cover to keep warm.

4 Heat remaining oil in a large frying pan on stove top; cook sausages for 2 minutes or until browned lightly. Transfer to baking dish with garlic; roast, in oven, for a further 10 minutes or until sausages are cooked through and garlic is soft. Cool sausages 10 minutes; slice thinly diagonally.

5 Cut garlic in half horizontally, squeeze flesh into a small bowl; add mayonnaise and juice, mash with a fork. Combine sausages and remaining ingredients with potato; toss well, season to taste. Divide potato salad among 12 x 1-cup boxes or containers; top with garlic mayonnaise.

do-ahead Potato salad can be made 8 hours ahead, minus the sausages; store, covered, in the fridge.

Tip Make your own lemon-infused extra virgin olive oil by combining extra virgin olive oil and finely grated lemon rind.

heirloom tomato and mozzarella salad

- 2 x 125g (4 ounces) long sourdough bread rolls
- 1 clove garlic, halved
- ¼ cup (60ml) olive oil
- 850g (1¾ pounds) small heirloom tomatoes, halved and quartered
- 220g (7 ounces) buffalo mozzarella, torn into small pieces

basil and lemon dressing

- 1 clove garlic, crushed
- 1 cup firmly packed fresh basil leaves
- 1 teaspoon white (granulated) sugar
- ¼ cup (60ml) white balsamic vinegar
- ½ cup (125ml) lemon-infused extra virgin olive oil

1 Make basil and lemon dressing.
2 Cut bread into 5mm (¼-inch) thick slices; rub both sides with cut side of garlic; brush with olive oil. Cook on a hot grill pan (or toast under grill/broiler) until browned lightly.
3 Combine tomato, cheese, toast, any remaining olive oil and dressing in a large bowl; toss to combine. Divide salad among 12 x 1-cup boxes or containers; sprinkle over extra fresh small basil leaves to serve, if you like.

basil and lemon dressing Blend or process ingredients until smooth; season to taste.

do-ahead Dressing can be prepared 8 hours ahead; store, covered, in the fridge.

serves 12
prep + cook time 25 minutes
nutritional count per serving 19.8g total fat (5.1g saturated fat); 1092kJ (260 cal); 12.4g carbohydrate; 7.4g protein; 1g fibre

Cocktails

barbados

Place 1½ cups caster (superfine) sugar in a large heavy-based frying pan over medium heat; cook, stirring, until a dark caramel colour. Carefully add 1 cup of water and the pulp of 8 passionfruit; when the bubbles subside, stir the mixture until smooth. Pour mixture into a large stainless steel bowl, add 750g (1½ pounds) thinly slice pineapple; turn to coat in mixture. Juice 3 medium oranges; cut 1 medium orange into slices. Add juice and slices to the bowl with 1 cup chilled dark rum and 2 cups lemonade; stir to combine. Fill one-third of a jug with crushed ice. Add rum and fruit mixture, serve immediately.

makes 1.5 litres (6 cups)
prep + cook time 25 minutes

tea party tipple

Trim 20cm (8-inch) stalk fresh lemon grass, cut in half lengthways; place in a heatproof jug. Add 2 earl grey tea bags, ⅓ cup caster (superfine) sugar and 1½ cups of boiling water, stir until sugar dissolves; stand 10 minutes. Discard tea bags; cover, refrigerate until cold. To serve, fill one-third of a jug with ice; add 1 medium thinly sliced lemon, tea mixture and lemon grass stalks. Stir in 600ml chilled bottled dry ginger ale, ⅓ cup lemon juice and 1 cup gin to combine.

makes 1.25 litres (5 cups)
prep time 15 minutes (+ refrigeration)

venice dusk

Cut rind from 1kg (2-pound) piece seedless watermelon; cut flesh into 2cm (¾-inch) cubes, place in a ziptop bag; freeze 1 hour or until ready to use. Half fill a jug with ice, frozen watermelon and 6 wide strips of mandarin rind. Stir 1 cup chilled vodka and ¼ cup caster (superfine) sugar in a small bowl until sugar dissolves; stir mixture into jug with 1 cup chilled Aperol or Campari, 3 cups chilled soda water, 1 cup strained mandarin juice and ⅓ cup strained lemon juice, serve immediately.

cucumber basil gimlet

Process 1¼ cups caster (superfine) sugar, 1 cup firmly packed fresh basil leaves and 5 chopped lebanese cucumbers until smooth. Fill a jug one-third full with crushed ice. Strain cucumber mixture through a fine sieve into jug, pushing down on solids to extract all liquid. Add 700ml chilled gin and ½ cup strained lime juice; stir well to combine. Top with ¼ cup fresh basil leaves and 1 thinly sliced lebanese cucumber.

tip Use a vegetable peeler to thinly slice the cucumber lengthways.

makes 2 litres (8 cups)
prep time 15 minutes (+ freezing)

makes 1.25 litres (5 cups)
prep time 15 minutes

five-spice squid with lime mayonnaise

- 2 tablespoons chinese five-spice
- 1 tablespoon ground ginger
- 1 teaspoon sea salt flakes, crushed
- 3 teaspoons onion powder
- 2 tablespoons self-raising flour
- ½ cup (75g) cornflour (cornstarch)
- 600g (1¼ pounds) cleaned small squid (hoods and tentacles)
- vegetable oil, for deep-frying
- 4 green onions (scallions), sliced thinly diagonally
- 2 fresh long red chillies, sliced thinly diagonally
- 4 limes, each cut into 6 wedges

lime mayonnaise

- 2 teaspoons finely grated lime rind
- 2 teaspoons lime juice
- 2 cups (600g) japanese mayonnaise

1 Make lime mayonnaise.
2 Combine spices, salt and onion powder in a large bowl; reserve one-third of spice mixture. Add flours to remaining mixture; stir to combine.
3 Cut each squid hood in half lengthways. Score inside in a criss-cross pattern with a sharp knife, then cut into 1.5cm (½-inch) wide strips.
4 Fill a large wok one-third full with oil; heat to 180°C/350°F (or until a cube of bread turns golden in 10 seconds). Toss squid in flour spice mix; shaking off excess. Deep fry, in batches, for 2 minutes or until golden and just tender. Remove squid with a slotted spoon; drain on paper towel. Transfer to a large bowl.
5 Fry onion and chilli for 2 minutes or until golden. Using a slotted spoon, remove from oil, add to bowl with squid; toss well to combine.
6 Divide squid into 24 x ¼-cup serving cones. Sprinkle with reserved spice mix, serve with lime wedges and lime mayonnaise.

lime mayonnaise
Combine ingredients in a small bowl. Cover, refrigerate until ready to serve.

do-ahead Recipe can be prepared a day ahead up to the end of step 3; store, covered, in the fridge.

serves 24
prep + cook time 40 minutes
nutritional count per serving 22g total fat (3.9g saturated fat); 987kJ (236 cal); 4.3g carbohydrate; 4.6g protein; 0.2g fibre

tip To clean squid, gently pull head and tentacles with internal sac away from body. Remove clear cartilage from inside body. Cut tentacles from head just below the eyes; discard head. Remove and discard side fins and skin from body with salted fingers. Wash the body and tentacles thoroughly; pat dry.

tip To make the curry go further, add an extra 200g (6½ ounces) each of fresh baby corn and trimmed green beans.

little thai green chicken curries

- 1½ cups (300g) jasmine rice
- 3 cups (750ml) water
- ¾ cup (30g) flaked coconut
- 2 tablespoons peanut or vegetable oil
- 800g (1½ pounds) chicken thigh fillets, trimmed
- 100g (3 ounces) green curry paste
- 1 clove garlic, crushed
- 1 tablespoon finely grated fresh ginger
- 225g (7 ounces) canned bamboo shoots, rinsed, drained
- 400g (12½ ounces) canned coconut cream
- 200g (6½ ounces) snow peas, trimmed, sliced thinly diagonally
- 1 tablespoon lime juice
- 1 cup coriander leaves (cilantro)
- 2 small red thai (serrano) chillies, halved, sliced thinly

serves 12
prep + cook time 50 minutes
nutritional count per serving 23.4g total fat (11.2g saturated fat); 1512kJ (361 cal); 23.6g carbohydrate; 13.5g protein; 1.2g fibre

1 Place rice in a sieve; rinse under running water until water runs clear. Place rice and the water in a medium saucepan; bring to the boil over medium heat. Reduce heat to low, cover with lid; cook for 12 minutes or until most of the water is absorbed. Stand, covered, for 10 minutes.

2 Meanwhile, place coconut in a medium frying pan; cook, stirring over high heat, for 4 minutes or until golden. Transfer to a medium bowl; cool.

3 Heat half the oil in a large wok over high heat. Add half the chicken; stir fry for 4 minutes or until browned and just cooked. Remove from wok. Repeat with remaining oil and chicken. Slice chicken thinly; cover to keep warm.

4 Add curry paste, garlic and ginger to wok; stir fry for 2 minutes or until heated through. Add bamboo shoots and coconut cream; bring to the boil. Reduce heat; simmer 3 minutes or until sauce thickens. Return chicken to wok. Stir in snow peas and juice; stir fry for a further 2 minutes.

5 Divide rice and curry between small boxes or containers, allowing ⅓ cup for each. Sprinkle over combined coriander, chilli and coconut to serve.

do-ahead All curry ingredients can be weighed and prepared up to 8 hours ahead; store, covered, in the fridge. Rice can be cooked 8 hours ahead; refrigerate immediately after cooking and reheat thoroughly.

Tip Ask the butcher to cut the ribs into racks of 5 when you buy them, or do it yourself using poultry shears; cut between each bone to separate into smaller racks.

smoky barbecued pork ribs

- ¾ cup (270g) honey
- 1½ tablespoons smoked paprika
- 1½ tablespoons wholegrain mustard
- 1½ cups (420g) HP sauce
- ¼ cup (55g) firmly packed brown sugar
- 2 cloves garlic, crushed
- 3kg (6½ pounds) American-style pork ribs, cut into racks of 5

1 Place honey, paprika, mustard, sauce, sugar and garlic in a large bowl; stir to combine. Add ribs to marinade; rub marinade all over ribs to coat. Cover; refrigerate 2 hours to allow flavours to penetrate.
2 Preheat oven to 180°C/350°F. Line a large roasting pan with baking paper.
3 Place ribs and marinade in baking pan; cover with foil. Bake 1 hour.

4 Remove ribs from oven; brush ribs with marinade from base of pan. Increase oven temperature to 220°C/425°F. Roast ribs, uncovered, for a further 5 minutes, basting occasionally, or until dark and sticky.
5 To serve, cut into individual ribs; place 5 ribs into each box or container.

do-ahead Ribs can be prepared up to the end of step 3; store, covered, in the fridge.

serves 10
prep + cook time
1 hour 30 minutes
(+ refrigeration)
**nutritional count per
serving** 11.9g total fat
(4.5g saturated fat);
1573kJ (376 cal);
38.9g carbohydrate;
28.7g protein; 0.6g fibre

AMERICAN-STYLE PORK RIBS
pork spare ribs that are sold
in long slabs or racks of 10 to
12 ribs, trimmed so that little
fat remains.

ANGOSTURA BITTERS brand
name of a type of aromatic
bitters, used mainly in drinks,
from aperitifs and cocktails
to digestifs, but also desserts
and savoury dishes. Its recipe
is a closely guarded secret,
but it is infused with many
herbs and spices.

BAMBOO SHOOTS the tender
shoots of the bamboo plant,
available in cans; must be
drained and rinsed before use.

BREAD
afghan a flatbread, similar
to lavash or naan breads;
can be rectangular or oval
in shape. Baked in a tandoor
oven, its texture is dense
enough that it is used to
pick up foods.

sourdough a low-risen bread
with a dense centre and crisp
crust; made from a yeast starter
culture used to make the
previous loaf of bread. May or
may not have a sour flavour.

tortillas thin, round unleavened
bread originating in Mexico.
Two kinds are available, one
made from wheat flour and the
other from corn (maize meal).

BREADCRUMBS
japanese also known as panko;
available in larger pieces and
fine crumbs; have a lighter
texture than Western-style
breadcrumbs. Gives a crunchy
texture with a delicate, pale
golden colour.

packaged fine-textured,
crunchy white breadcrumbs.

BUTTERMILK originally the
term given to the slightly
sour liquid left after butter
was churned from cream,
today it is commercially
made similarly to yoghurt.
Sold alongside fresh dairy
products in supermarkets;
despite the implication of
its name, it is low in fat.

BUTTERNUT PUMPKIN
(squash) a member of the
gourd family. Butternut is
pear-shaped with a golden
skin and orange flesh.

CAPERS the grey-green buds
of a warm climate (usually
Mediterranean) shrub, sold
either dried and salted or
pickled in a vinegar brine.
Baby capers, those picked
early, are fuller-flavoured,
smaller and more expensive
than the full-sized ones.
Capers, whether packed in
brine or in salt, must be
rinsed well before using.

CHEESE
blue mould-treated cheeses
mottled with blue veining.
Varieties include firm and
crumbly stilton types and
mild, creamy brie-like cheeses.

bocconcini from the
diminutive of "boccone",
meaning mouthful in Italian;
walnut-sized, baby mozzarella,
a delicate, semi-soft, white
cheese traditionally made
from buffalo milk. Sold fresh,
it spoils rapidly so will only
keep, refrigerated in brine,
for 1 or 2 days at the most.

cheddar the most common
cow-milk tasty cheese; should
be aged, hard and have a
pronounced bite.

cream commonly known as
philadelphia or philly; a soft
cow-milk cheese with a fat
content ranging from 14 to
33 per cent.

fetta Greek in origin; a
crumbly textured goat- or
sheep-milk cheese with a
sharp salty taste. Ripened
and stored in salted whey.

gruyère a hard-rind Swiss
cheese with small holes and a
nutty, slightly salty flavour. A
popular cheese for soufflés.

haloumi a Greek Cypriot
cheese having a semi-firm,
spongy texture and very salty
yet sweet flavour. Ripened
and stored in salted whey;
it's best grilled or fried, and
holds its shape well on being
heated. Should be eaten
while still warm as it becomes
tough and rubbery on cooling.

mozzarella soft, spun-curd
cheese; originating in
southern Italy where it was
traditionally made from
water-buffalo milk. Now
generally manufactured
from cow milk, it is the most
popular pizza cheese because
of its low melting point and
elasticity when heated (used
for texture rather than flavour).

parmesan also known as
parmigiano; a hard, grainy
cow-milk cheese. The curd
is salted in brine for a month
before being aged for up to
2 years.

glossary

persian fetta a soft, creamy fetta marinated in a blend of olive oil, garlic, herbs and spices. It is available from most larger supermarkets.

CHICKEN

tenderloin thin tender strip of meat lying just under the breast.

thigh fillet skin and bone removed.

wing nibbles pre-cut chicken wing and drumstick pieces; if unavailable use chicken drumettes.

CHILLI

jalapeño hot green chillies, available bottled, in brine, or fresh from specialty greengrocers.

long red available both fresh and dried; a generic term used for any moderately hot, long, thin chilli (about 6cm to 8cm long).

red thai also known as 'scuds'; small, very hot and bright red in colour.

CHINESE COOKING WINE also known as shao hsing or chinese rice wine. Found in Asian food shops; substitute with mirin or sherry.

CORIANDER also known as cilantro, a bright-green-leafed herb that is also available ground or as seeds; do not substitute either of these for fresh, as the tastes are completely different.

CORNFLOUR also known as cornstarch; used as a thickening agent in cooking. Available as 100% maize (corn) and wheaten cornflour.

CORNICHON a very small variety of pickled cucumber; when pickled with dill they are known as a dill pickle. Available from most major supermarkets and delicatessens.

CREAM we use fresh cream, also known as pouring, single and pure cream; it has no additives.

sour a thick, commercially cultured soured cream.

CRÈME FRAÎCHE mature fermented cream having a slightly tangy, nutty flavour and velvety texture.

DUKKAH an Egyptian spice blend made with roasted nuts and aromatic spices. It is available from Middle-Eastern food stores, specialty spice stores and some larger supermarkets.

ELDERFLOWER CORDIAL an infusion of elderberry flowers and sugar syrup. Available from some delicatessens. Can be substituted with orange, lemon or lime cordial.

FIRM WHITE FISH FILLET blue eye, bream, flathead, swordfish, ling, whiting, jewfish, snapper or sea perch are all good choices. Check for any small bones and use tweezers to remove them.

FLOUR

plain an all-purpose flour made from wheat.

self-raising (rising) plain or wholemeal flour combined with baking powder in the proportion of 1 cup flour to 2 teaspoons baking powder.

JUNIPER BERRIES the dried fruit from the evergreen tree of the same name, found in specialty spice stores and bigger delicatessens. Used to flavour gin.

LAMB

backstrap the larger fillet from a row of loin chops or cutlets.

cutlets small, tender rib chop.

MAYONNAISE we use mayonnaise made with whole eggs in our recipes.

japanese made using rice vinegar or apple cider vinegar, along with a small amount of mustard and MSG. It is generally richer in taste than Western-style mayonnaise.

MICRO HERBS harvested as the tiny first leaves emerge; used as both a visual and flavour component.

MIRIN a Japanese champagne-coloured cooking wine; made from glutinous rice and alcohol and used only for cooking. Should not be confused with sake.

MIZUNA a frizzy green salad leaf, Japanese in origin, with a delicate mustard flavour. Available from greengrocers and supermarkets.

MUSTARD

dijon a pale brown, distinctively flavoured, fairly mild french mustard.

english an extremely hot powdered mustard containing ground mustard seeds (both black or brown and yellow-white), wheat flour and turmeric. Also available in a milder, less hot, version.

wholegrain also known as seeded. A french-style coarse-grain mustard made from crushed mustard seeds and dijon-style french mustard.

OIL

cooking spray we use a cholesterol-free cooking spray made from canola oil.

olive made from ripened olives. Extra virgin and virgin are the first and second press, respectively, of the olives and are therefore considered the best; the "extra light" or "light" name on other types refers to taste not fat levels.

peanut pressed from ground peanuts; the most commonly used oil in Asian cooking because of its high smoke point (capacity to handle high heat without burning).

sesame made from roasted, crushed, white sesame seeds; a flavouring rather than a cooking medium.

PANCETTA Italian bacon that is cured but not smoked.

PAPRIKA a ground dried sweet red capsicum; many types are available, including sweet, hot, mild and smoked.

PARSLEY, FLAT-LEAF also known as continental parsley or italian parsley; stronger in flavour and darker in colour than other varieties.

PIRI PIRI (peri peri) a hot chilli sauce used in Portuguese, African and Brazilian cookery.

PROSCIUTTO an unsmoked Italian ham; salted, air-cured and aged, it is usually eaten uncooked.

PROSECCO sparkling Italian wine. Available from selected bottle shops, or substitute with any dry sparkling wine.

SAUCE

HP a blend of tomatoes, malt vinegar, molasses, dates, tamarind and spices.

soy also known as sieu, made from fermented soya beans. Several variations are available in most supermarkets and Asian food stores.

sweet chilli comparatively mild, fairly sticky and runny bottled sauce made from red chillies, sugar, garlic and white vinegar; used in Thai cooking and as a condiment.

tamari a thick, dark soy sauce made mainly from soya beans without the wheat used in standard soy sauce.

tomato also known as ketchup or catsup; a condiment made from tomatoes, vinegar and spices.

worcestershire thin, dark-brown spicy sauce developed by the British when in India; used as a seasoning for meat, gravies and cocktails, and as a condiment.

SNOW PEAS also called mange tout; a variety of garden pea, eaten pod and all (although you may need to string them).

SUGAR

brown a finely granulated, extremely soft sugar retaining molasses for its characteristic colour and flavour.

caster also known as superfine or finely granulated table sugar.

palm also known as jaggery or gula melaka; made from the sap of the sugar palm tree. Light brown to dark brown in colour and usually sold in rock-hard cakes; substitute with brown sugar if unavailable.

white coarsely granulated table sugar, also known as crystal sugar.

SUMAC a purple-red, astringent spice ground from berries growing in the Mediterranean; it has a tart, lemony flavour.

TAHINI sesame seed paste; available from Middle-Eastern food stores. Most often used in hummus, baba ghanoush and other Lebanese recipes.

VINEGAR

balsamic originally from Modena, Italy, there are now many balsamic vinegars on the market ranging in pungency and quality.

red wine based on fermented red wine.

rice wine made from rice wine lees (sediment left after fermentation), salt and alcohol.

white wine made from a blend of white wines.

WONTON WRAPPERS also known as wonton skins; they come in varying thicknesses. Found in the refrigerated section of supermarkets; gow gee, egg or spring roll pastry sheets can be substituted.

YOGHURT, GREEK-STYLE full-cream yoghurt often made from sheep milk; the milk liquids are drained off leaving a thick, smooth consistency with a tart taste.

conversion chart

measures

One Australian metric measuring cup holds approximately 250ml, one Australian metric tablespoon holds 20ml, one Australian metric teaspoon holds 5ml. The difference between one country's measuring cups and another's is within a 2- or 3-teaspoon variance, and will not affect your cooking results. North America, New Zealand and the United Kingdom use a 15ml tablespoon. All cup and spoon measurements are level. The most accurate way of measuring dry ingredients is to weigh them. When measuring liquids, use a clear glass or plastic jug with metric markings. We use large eggs with an average weight of 60g.

dry measures

METRIC	IMPERIAL
15g	½oz
30g	1oz
60g	2oz
90g	3oz
125g	4oz (¼lb)
155g	5oz
185g	6oz
220g	7oz
250g	8oz (½lb)
280g	9oz
315g	10oz
345g	11oz
375g	12oz (¾lb)
410g	13oz
440g	14oz
470g	15oz
500g	16oz (1lb)
750g	24oz (1½lb)
1kg	32oz (2lb)

liquid measures

METRIC	IMPERIAL
30ml	1 fluid oz
60ml	2 fluid oz
100ml	3 fluid oz
125ml	4 fluid oz
150ml	5 fluid oz
190ml	6 fluid oz
250ml	8 fluid oz
300ml	10 fluid oz
500ml	16 fluid oz
600ml	20 fluid oz
1000ml (1 litre)	1¾ pints

length measures

METRIC	IMPERIAL
3mm	⅛in
6mm	¼in
1cm	½in
2cm	¾in
2.5cm	1in
5cm	2in
6cm	2½in
8cm	3in
10cm	4in
13cm	5in
15cm	6in
18cm	7in
20cm	8in
23cm	9in
25cm	10in
28cm	11in
30cm	12in (1ft)

oven temperatures

These oven temperatures are only a guide for conventional ovens. For fan-forced ovens, check the manufacturer's manual.

	°C (CELSIUS)	°F (FAHRENHEIT)
Very slow	120	250
Slow	150	275-300
Moderately slow	160	325
Moderate	180	350-375
Moderately hot	200	400
Hot	220	425-450
Very hot	240	475

The imperial measurements used in these recipes are approximate only. Measurements for cake pans are approximate only. Using same-shaped cake pans of a similar size should not affect the outcome of your baking. We measure the inside top of the cake pan to determine sizes.

index

This book is published in 2014 by Octopus Publishing Group Limited
based on materials licensed to it by Bauer Media Books, Australia
Bauer Media Books are published by Bauer Media Pty Limited
54 Park St, Sydney; GPO Box 4088, Sydney, NSW 2001, Australia
phone (+61) 2 9282 8618; fax (+61) 2 9126 3702
www.awwcookbooks.com.au

MEDIA GROUP

BAUER MEDIA BOOKS

Publisher - Jo Runciman

Editorial & Food Director - Pamela Clark

Director of Sales, Marketing & Rights - Brian Cearnes

Creative Director - Hieu Chi Nguyen

Art Director - Hannah Blackmore

Designer - Melissa Dumas

Junior Editor - Amy Bayliss

Food Concept Director - Sophia Young

Food Editor - Emma Braz

Published and Distributed in the United Kingdom by Octopus Publishing Group

Endeavour House

189 Shaftesbury Avenue

London WC2H 8JY

phone (+44)(0)207 632 5400; fax (+44)(0)207 632 5405

info@octopus-publishing.co.uk;

www.octopusbooks.co.uk

Printed by 1010 Printing International Limited in China.

International foreign language rights, Brian Cearnes, Bauer Media Books
bcearnes@bauer-media.com.au

A catalogue record for this book is available from the British Library.
ISBN: 978 1 74245 447 4

© Bauer Media Pty Limited 2014
ABN 18 053 273 546